PUFFIN BOOKS

THE BORROWERS

Mr Potter got his stethoscope and listened to the wall. A moment later he grinned, poking his pudgy finger at the wall. 'There!' he said.

Jeff whacked at the wall with the hammer's claw.

Inside the wall the gigantic claw of the hammer suddenly plunged through the plaster just inches away from Arrietty and Peagreen. They screamed and started to run.

Outside the wall Mr Potter kept pointing and yelling, 'There! There!'

Each time, Jeff smashed a big hole in the wall with his hammer, and each time, the hammer narrowly missed Arrietty and Peagreen.

Inside, the Borrower children reached a wooden wall support and froze, panting hard. Jeff went right on hammering, faster and faster, until he'd smashed a big hole in the wall.

Also available

THE BORROWERS STORYBOOK
THE BORROWERS DELUXE STORYBOOK

Some books by Mary Norton

THE BORROWERS (*Original story*)
THE BORROWERS AFIELD
THE BORROWERS AFLOAT
THE BORROWERS ALOFT
THE BORROWERS AVENGED
THE COMPLETE BORROWERS STORIES

BEDKNOB AND BROOMSTICK

The Borrowers

A novelization by
Sherwood Smith

Based on the screenplay by
Gavin Scott and John Kamps

Based on the novels by
Mary Norton

PUFFIN BOOKS

PUFFIN BOOKS

Published by the Penguin Group
Penguin Books Ltd, 27 Wrights Lane, London W8 5TZ, England
Penguin Books USA Inc., 375 Hudson Street, New York, New York 10014, USA
Penguin Books Australia Ltd, Ringwood, Victoria, Australia
Penguin Books Canada Ltd, 10 Alcorn Avenue, Toronto, Ontario, Canada M4V 3B2
Penguin Books (NZ) Ltd, 182–190 Wairau Road, Auckland 10, New Zealand

Penguin Books Ltd, Registered Offices: Harmondsworth, Middlesex, England

First published in the USA by Harcourt Brace & Company 1997
Published in Great Britain in Puffin Books 1997
3 5 7 9 10 8 6 4 2

Puffin Film and TV Tie-in edition first published 1997

Set in Baskerville MT
Typeset by Rowland Phototypesetting Ltd,
Bury St Edmunds, Suffolk
Made and printed in England by Clays Ltd, St Ives plc

British Library Cataloguing in Publication Data
A CIP catalogue record for this book is available from the British Library

ISBN 0-140-39049-9

ONE

ONCE UPON A TIME there was a boy named Pete Lender, who lived with his mother and father in a big old house in the middle of a little town. Pete and his parents, Joe and Victoria Lender, really liked the old house, which had once belonged to Victoria's aunt.

Not long after they moved in, Pete began to notice some strange things.

One evening his father came into his room in time to see Pete crouched on the floor, watching a wind-up toy march towards a mousetrap. Set in the trap was a grape.

The toy walked straight into the trap. *Snick! Clatter!* SPLAT! The toy smashed into pieces and the grape squished. Pete looked up and grinned.

'Pete,' Joe Lender said, 'have you seen my glasses?'

Pete's dad was a nice guy but very absent-minded. 'Look on your face!'

Joe felt his face – and smiled when he found the glasses. 'What about my brown socks?' he added hopefully.

'Did you check your feet?' Pete asked, resetting his trap.

Joe almost looked, then he sighed. 'Very funny.' He wandered out again, and Pete could hear him calling, 'Honey, I can't find my brown socks.'

'Wear the black ones,' Pete heard his mother call from the utility room, and a moment later she yelled, '*Ow!* PETE!'

Pete picked up his trap and ran downstairs, pausing to set the trap by the first step. In the utility room, he found his mother holding her hand out stiffly. Her fingers had been caught in a trap. He sprang the trap and Victoria freed her fingers.

'What is it you're hoping to catch?' she asked, trying not to be angry.

'I'm not sure,' Pete admitted.

Victoria held up her hands. There were bandages all over them. 'Can't we keep my fingers out of it?' she pleaded.

'I'm sorry.' Pete felt bad about his mother's fingers. 'But there has to be a reason we can't find anything in this house.'

'There is,' Victoria said with a smile. 'It's called your father.'

'What about the pen by the phone, those missing Christmas tree lights, your needle and thread, the safety pins and dental floss and matches?'

'OK, OK,' Victoria said, leading the way to the kitchen.

'Something is taking our stuff, and I'm going to find out what it is,' Pete promised.

Victoria took a lipstick and mirror from her handbag just as Joe wandered back in. Pete realized they had their 'going out' clothes on. 'Where are you two going?'

'We have a meeting with the great Ocious P. Potter,' Joe said.

'What's so great about him?'

'He's a lawyer,' Victoria said. 'We have to see him about the house.'

‘Is something wrong?’ Pete was immediately worried.

Joe shook his head, looking around with a vague expression on his face. ‘He probably wants us to sign some papers. I’m sure it’s nothing.’

Victoria looked at the clock. ‘Let’s go, Pete. You’re going to be late for school.’

‘I can’t find my stupid keys,’ Joe began, searching his pockets.

Victoria put her hands up to her face as if she was horrified. ‘Oh my!’ she exclaimed. ‘I’m so sorry, Pete. You’re right. Some – some – thing must have taken them!’

‘See!’ Pete exclaimed in triumph.

Victoria picked up the keys and held them out in front of Pete and Joe, laughing.

‘Very funny,’ Pete said as all three of them went out of the door.

Joe and Victoria got into their car and drove off. Pete climbed on his bike and began to ride, but he kept looking back at the house.

Inside the utility room the spin-dryer door mysteriously opened just a crack and a towel dropped out, floating down to the laundry basket. Then above the dryer, one by one, a shelf full of old cookery books began to fall as though pushed from behind.

Bang! SNAP! Pete's trap sprang once again.

'Gotcha!' Pete's head popped up outside the window. He tried to look in, and when he couldn't see his trap he disappeared.

A few moments later he raced into the house, pausing only to check the traps he'd set by the stairs, and on the shelves, and in the wardrobes before he dashed into the utility room. On the floor he saw his sprung trap – empty.

The bait was gone. Next to the trap were a few grey hairs.

'A mouse?' Pete was puzzled and a little disappointed.

He reset his trap and left for school.

TWO

PETE AND HIS PARENTS had truly gone.

In the kitchen, near the floor, the heater grate slowly swung out and a tiny man appeared. He was no more than six inches tall. He tossed up to the table a hook made from a paper clip. *Clank!* The hook caught on the milk jug. Attached to it was a white rope – dental floss – up which the little man climbed.

He reached the top of the table and looked around. The little man's name was Pod Clock. He was about Joe Lender's age. In one hand he carried a stick with lots of attachments – including a fake mouse's foot. This he patted as he looked down at one of Pete's traps. 'Gets 'em every time,' he said happily.

He checked around again, then slid down his

rope to the back of a kitchen chair, where he balanced carefully before throwing his hook across to the counter. He tightrope-walked across his rope and sat down on the counter to wipe his face.

'I'm getting too old for this,' he said.

But a moment later he got up again, this time moving to the electric mixer. He hooked his rope round the beater blades and threw the other end over the edge of the counter. Then he tugged the mixer dial down to the lowest speed.

The machine whirred quietly, the blades turned, the rope wound up – and a lift made out of an empty yoghurt pot appeared at the edge. Out popped Arrietty Clock, Pod's daughter. She was a bit older than Pete Lender.

'Now stop right there, Arrietty,' Pod said. 'What's the First Rule of Borrowing?'

Arrietty grinned at her father. 'The First Rule of Borrowing?' she said in a teasing voice. 'Hmmm. That's a tricky one. Is it, "Have as much fun as you can"?'

'Arrietty!'

Arrietty sighed and recited by heart, '"The

First Rule of Borrowing is that a Borrower must never be seen." You've only told me a zillion times. But I checked and the coast was clear. Can we go now?'

'Hold on. Peagreen!'

Pod looked down into the yoghurt pot, where Arrietty's brother was sitting lazily. He was younger than Pete, about five years old.

'Come on, Peagreen. We have a big day ahead of us,' Pod said.

'I hate big days,' Peagreen whined, dragging himself up.

'You hate everything,' Arrietty said in disgust.

'That's not true,' Peagreen said as he followed them along the counter. 'I like sweets. Chocolate. Desserts –'

Pod interrupted. 'What's Rule Number Two?'

All three – even Peagreen – worked as they talked, stocking up on cornflakes, peanuts and rice.

'"Rule Two,"' Arrietty and Peagreen said together, '"is that Borrowers never borrow more than they need."'

'Unless it's chocolate,' Peagreen added.

'Some Borrowers take more than they need. Did I ever tell you about the time my old friend Swag borrowed an entire banana from a human bean's picnic?'

'Only about a million times,' Arrietty said.

'Tell us the bit about eating nothing but banana for a month,' Peagreen urged.

Pod grinned, looking back in memory. 'Ah yes, Swag was special. Of course, your mother couldn't stand him. Something to do with the smell of drains.'

As her father talked, Arrietty looked around the kitchen. On the door of the refrigerator was a picture of Pete, Victoria and Joe.

When Pod paused to pack some instant coffee, Arrietty said, 'Are beans *really* all that bad? Have Borrowers ever spoken to a bean?'

Pod looked sternly at his daughter. 'If a Borrower ever had the misfortune to meet a bean, the last thing he'd see would be a shoe. Then, *squish*!'

Arrietty pointed at the picture of Pete. 'The young bean looks nice.'

'Young beans are the worst of all. They still believe what they see,' Pod said as he heaved himself up and strapped an AA-size battery to his back. On Pod the battery was as big as a scuba-diving air tank. 'I needed a new battery. You two stay here and finish packing. Arrietty –'

'Yes, Papa?'

'Promise me you'll stay out of trouble.'

'I promise,' Arrietty said.

Peagreen made a face. He could see that, behind her back, Arrietty's fingers were crossed.

THREE

MEANWHILE, JOE AND VICTORIA sat in the rich fancy office of Ocious P. Potter, Attorney-at-Law.

Joe and Victoria were both upset. Mr Potter, however, was in a good mood.

Everyone in town called Mr Potter a Great Man, and a handsome one as well – and if they forgot, he was the first to remind them. No one thought more highly of Mr Potter than Ocious P. Potter himself. He was tall and pudgy with a round face. He wore a very expensive suit, and his moustache was neatly clipped. On his fingers were expensive rings. He dressed like a Great Man, because he had Ambition.

'No will?' Joe and Victoria were saying together.

Mr Potter tried to look sad. 'Believe me, I've searched for it. Your aunt's will doesn't exist.'

'But we were here, in this office, when Aunt Mary said she was leaving the house to us! You were sitting right there!'

Mr Potter shrugged, still trying to look sympathetic as he lit up a big, smelly cigar. 'Sometimes people say one thing then turn round and do the opposite. Or, in your aunt's case, they turn round and drop dead.' He started stacking papers on his desk. 'Since your aunt died without leaving a will, I am left with the sad and expensive task of settling her debts by selling the house.'

Victoria looked surprised. 'She had debts? She always had plenty of money before she died.'

Mr Potter shrugged again. 'There were fees – lots of fees. *My* fees. Then there were some overdue library books, and it appears she had a taste for those chocolates. You know, the ones with the stuff inside –'

'She loved that house, and so do we. We promised we would always take good care of it,' Joe protested. 'Can't we work something out?'

'I already have.' Mr Potter rose from his tall

leather chair and moved to something sitting on a table, hidden by a dark cloth. 'The world is a fast train speeding towards the future, and I don't want our little town to get left behind.'

He whipped away the dark cloth, revealing a model of a tall, ugly apartment building. 'Twenty-four highly expensive apartments in the place of one old house,' Mr Potter said, grinning with pride. 'Phase One of my plan to make this town into something BIG.'

'You're demolishing our house for *that*?' Joe gasped.

'Nice, isn't it?' Mr Potter asked, and then his smile disappeared. 'You have until Saturday to get out.'

'Saturday?' Victoria asked, her eyes prickling with tears.

Mr Potter held up his hands, wrists together, as if they were handcuffed, meaning that there was nothing he could do about it. 'Where there's no will,' he said, his sympathy now so fake that even Joe noticed, 'there's no way.'

A few minutes later, Mr Potter watched through his office window as Joe and Victoria walked slowly out of the building.

'Couldn't we talk to someone?' Victoria was saying sadly.

'You heard him. If there's no will . . .' Joe looked even sadder.

'Pete's going to take this very hard,' Victoria said.

Grinning smugly, Mr Potter turned away from the window and walked back to his model apartment building. It was really, really ugly, but Mr Potter was very, very proud of it. He took out a little model sign and put it on the top of the building. The sign said POTTERSVILLE.

'Today, Potter's apartments,' the lawyer said, gloating. 'Tomorrow, Pottersville!'

FOUR

BACK IN THE KITCHEN of the Lenders' house, Arrietty and Peagreen were still sitting on the counter where Pod had told them to wait.

But not for long.

Arrietty started climbing up the refrigerator which, to someone her size, was as large and scary as a big ice-white cliff. She used the magnetic alphabet letters as footholds.

Peagreen watched, horrified. 'Where are you going?' he asked after a time. 'Dad told us not to budge.'

'That was his first mistake,' Arrietty said.

Peagreen began to sing, just like little brothers everywhere. 'Dad's going to KILL you, Dad's going to KILL you!'

'Fine,' Arrietty said. 'If you won't help me, then I'll eat all the ice cream myself.'

'Ice cream? What's ice cream?' Peagreen demanded.

Arrietty grinned. 'Just a sweet, creamy, chocolate dessert that melts its cool, velvety way down your throat. I don't think you'd like it.'

Peagreen jumped up and started climbing even faster than his sister.

Before long they reached the top of the fridge and, by wedging an ice-lolly stick into the door, they managed to get the freezer open. Then, in typical bossy, big-sister fashion, Arrietty said, 'Your job is to make sure the door stays open so I can get out again. My job is to climb inside, explore and generally have a good time.'

Peagreen said, 'Arrietty – '

'What?'

'I'm going to need a lot of that stuff!'

Arrietty disappeared inside the freezer. She looked around. All those packages of vegetables and TV dinners – it was like a wonderland to her. 'Look, a whole room full of winter,' she said to herself as she made her way to the ice cream.

'What's it like in there?' Peagreen called down to her.

'It's just like that Christmas card we borrowed.'

With some difficulty she prised loose the top of the ice cream, then buried her hands in the chocolate.

Up above, Peagreen got suspicious when he couldn't hear his sister's steps crunching around on the icy shelves. 'Arrietty? Have you found it yet?'

Arrietty yelled back with her mouth full, 'I'm sure it must be around here somewhere!'

'Hurry up, Arrietty. I'm sure –' Peagreen stopped when his hand slipped and the ice-lolly stick fell into the freezer.

The door slammed shut.

Inside, Arrietty saw the door close and the light suddenly go out. Peagreen, who had leant forward to try to catch the stick, got his arm stuck in the freezer door. 'Dad!' he screamed, 'HELP!'

Across the room Pod had got his battery and was just putting the radio back together. He peered across the vast space of the kitchen and saw his son trapped in the top of the fridge door, which for Borrowers was like being caught on the top of a sixty-storey building.

Using his stick full of gadgets and his dental-floss rope, Pod vaulted, somersaulted, climbed, jumped and slid around the kitchen until he reached Peagreen. Quickly he pulled him free.

'It's all *her* fault,' Peagreen said – of course – for Borrower children are pretty much like 'bean' children. '*She* made me do it!'

'And where is she?' Pod demanded.

Peagreen pointed to the freezer. 'Is that bad?'

'I don't think it could get much worse,' Pod began to grumble, but then they both froze.

The front door slammed. Pod and Peagreen looked at each other: the beans were back!

'It just got worse,' Pod said.

And he grabbed Peagreen under his arm and jumped over the edge of the fridge.

FIVE

'YAAAAAGH!' PEAGREEN YELLED.

Clink! Pod's hook caught on the handle of a frying pan on a nearby shelf, and the two of them rode gently down the dental-floss line to the counter.

'Go on home, son,' Pod whispered to Peagreen. 'Tell your mother not to worry.'

Peagreen hobbled off, looking back several times. Pod ran to the toaster and used all his weight to pull the lever down. Then he climbed up on to it.

Joe and Victoria entered the hallway. Both were very glum. Victoria sighed as she looked round. She loved the house, with its funky wallpaper and worn floors and comfy furniture. Her aunt had wanted the family to be here, and Victoria didn't want to leave!

Clack! Was that the toaster she heard?

She and Joe walked into the kitchen. Joe was puzzled too. He'd heard the sound but didn't know what it was. As both of them turned to look at the toaster, they missed the little figure who arced through the air, somersaulted and landed softly on the ice dispenser on the refrigerator door. There was no bread in the toaster, so Victoria and Joe forgot about the noise. They had too much else to worry about just now.

Seeing them turn away, Pod whispered into the ice dispenser, 'Now listen carefully. The beans are back. Find the round hole in the winter room.'

Inside the freezer, poor Arrietty felt her way carefully over the frozen foods. She was shivering terribly.

Victoria dropped sadly into a chair. 'What will we do?' she said.

'I don't know. Potter's given us so little time.' Joe reached for the radio, turned it on – and nothing happened. 'I can't believe this is dead,' he said. 'Didn't I just change the battery?'

Pod patted the battery on his pack, then he whispered up the ice-dispenser funnel, 'When I give the word, jump!'

'Maybe Mr Potter will have a change of heart,' Victoria said without much hope.

'You'd have to have a heart for that,' Joe answered as he took two glasses out of the cupboard.

'Now!' Pod said.

Arrietty bumped and slid her way down the long ice chute. Despite the danger, and how cold it was, she started grinning. *This was fun!*

She plopped out on to the ice-dispenser tray. 'Are you cross with me, Dad?'

Pod didn't have time to answer. They felt a shadow approach and saw two giant glasses coming right towards them, held in Joe's hands. The Borrowers pressed themselves back, but Arrietty was stuck right under the ice dispenser. Joe pressed the button, not seeing the Borrowers, and waited – but Pod had stuck his stick up to block the ice. Joe was puzzled. He turned away in order to hand a glass to Victoria.

'I think it would be best if you told Pete,'

Victoria said. 'You're so good at the father–son kind of thing.'

'No,' Joe said, turning back to look at the fridge. He opened the freezer door, found nothing wrong and shrugged. 'You're his mother. You should tell him.'

'Coward,' Victoria said with a smile.

'Wimp,' Joe said back. Now he looked at the ice dispenser. Nothing wrong there either – except this time, when he turned away, twenty ice cubes suddenly tumbled out and landed on the kitchen floor.

Joe bent down, now thoroughly puzzled. He picked up a tiny stick with dental floss hanging from it and tried to figure out where *that* had come from.

While he looked at it, Pod and Arrietty raced through special tunnels in the walls until they reached the floor. Underneath the floorboards the Clocks had built themselves a cosy little home out of all the odds and ends that they had borrowed from the house. It was lit by the very same string of Christmas tree lights that Pete had reported missing.

'I've been sick with worry,' Arrietty and Peagreen's mother, Homily, cried after hugging them both. 'How could you do this to me?' And to Pod she said, 'I told you they were too young to go borrowing.'

Arrietty wasn't listening. She whispered to Peagreen, 'I passed a mountain of peas. And there in front of me was a huge lake of ice cream. Chocolate ice cream.'

'You naughty girl, you could have been squished,' Homily scolded. And to Pod, 'You know, of course, who she takes after.'

'Me?' Pod sighed.

Arrietty mumbled, 'If I took after *him* I'd never have any fun.'

'Don't you believe it,' Homily said with a little smile. 'Your father was quite a rogue in his time.'

'My dad?' Arrietty said. 'His idea of a wild night is reciting safety rules.'

'No,' Homily said. 'You're just like your father was. He and his friends. They could never stay put for a minute. Oh, they were a horrible lot! Minty Branch, Swag Moss . . .' She held her nose. 'And that stinky Dustbunny Bin.' She sighed. 'I lost count of the times they almost got "seen".'

Pod said, 'I gave up my wild ways when I married your mother. She comes from very proper Borrowers. Much safer, they are.'

Arrietty said wistfully, 'I'll bet it was fun in the old days.'

'The old days.' Homily smiled. 'You should have seen this house back then. Old houses are best for Borrowers, and this one was full to the rafters. There were the Overmantels, the Furnaces, the Rafters . . .'

Arrietty said in disappointment, 'Now all those Borrowers families are gone and there's just us. No one to talk to, no one to meet. It's boring.'

Homily nodded in agreement. 'Of course, the social scene just hasn't been the same since they put in Central Eating.'

The whole family knew about Central Eating, which had forced so many Borrower families to move away. 'Black Tuesday,' Arrietty said.

Peagreen added importantly – showing off, Arrietty thought – 'It would have been Black Monday, but the plumber turned up a day late.'

'We can't be the only ones left,' Arrietty exclaimed.

'Of course not,' Pod said. 'Meanwhile, your mother is right about danger. And we should keep you at home for a while.'

'That's not fair!'

'At least until that awful young bean stops setting those traps everywhere.' Homily gave a nervous look round.

'You put us in danger, Arrietty. "A Borrower is quiet, alert, never seen, never heard,"' Pod added in a serious voice.

'It's the Borrower Way,' Homily added sternly.

'Borrower this, Borrower that,' Arrietty grumbled. 'I've lived in this house all my life and never seen another Borrower –'

Just then a terrible noise stopped them all.

'It's not Thursday, is it?' Pod asked, looking up at the ceiling. Right above their ceiling was the floor of the beans' hallway.

The noise got louder and more terrible. On the table the dishes began to vibrate, then the furniture.

'Have they changed the schedule?' Homily

said, racing about, trying to keep things from falling.

'Emergency stations, everyone!' Pod yelled.

They all strapped themselves into their chairs as the furniture jumped and thumped. The noise sounded like the world ending.

On the floor above them, Victoria was busy vacuuming the carpet.

When she reached the spot right over the Clocks' living area, the Borrowers watched their silverware and napkins fly up and stick to the ceiling. A moment later Peagreen started rising from his chair – he hadn't tied himself in properly. The others caught him by the ankles and, when the vacuum passed by at last, he fell on to the table with a thump.

They rose shakily and put things to rights again.

Later, after they had all eaten and darkness had fallen, the two young Borrowers were sent off to sleep.

Arrietty spent a few minutes in her room, bored.

After a while she got up again, looking round determinedly. She lit a bit of candle, then marched up to a picture of Queen Victoria, which was really just a postage stamp. She pulled the picture out – and beyond it was a hole, just large enough for a small Borrower to crawl through.

Without any hesitation she popped into the hole and let the picture fall back behind her.

SIX

JOE AND VICTORIA WAITED until after dinner before telling Pete the bad news.

'But this is *our* house,' Pete protested.

'It seems to belong to Mr Potter now,' his dad said.

'We'll have to find somewhere else to live,' his mother added.

'You two can do what you want. I'm staying here,' Pete said firmly.

'You can't,' Victoria said gently. 'They're going to tear the house down.'

'No!' Pete yelled, getting up and running out. 'I won't let them!'

Behind him he heard his father say, 'That went well.'

It was a joke, of course, meant to make everyone feel a little better, but Pete did not feel better. He loved this house! It was big and old and interesting, and he had his mystery to solve about the missing things.

Missing things – he stopped and scanned his room. All his toys were neatly put away and everything seemed to be where it belonged. His dresser was untouched, his bed made. Nothing out of place, except –

He looked at his chess set. A rook was missing!

He dashed across the room and looked more closely. All the chess pieces except the rook were sitting right in the middle of their squares, just where he had put them. So where was the rook?

Just then a light glowed through the cracks in his floor, but he didn't see it.

He looked round, then yanked open his wardrobe and burrowed inside. He *knew* he hadn't lost that chess piece, he knew it. Rubber bands, paper clips, pencils, those were things a person could lose. But not a chess piece.

He started throwing things out of his wardrobe, then stopped when he saw a tiny light glowing in the wall. Moving slowly and quietly, he leant forward and pressed his eye to a crack in the wardrobe wall. Inside he saw a tiny candle flame – but a moment later it was gone, as if someone had blown it out!

'Pete? Lost something?'

It was his father.

Pete backed out of the wardrobe – and Arrietty popped out from the wall and climbed on to his bookshelf.

His father held something out. 'Looking for this?'

Pete took the miniature stick from his father. There were teeny-tiny gadgets on it and string dangled down from it. 'I guess it's from one of my army men,' he said slowly.

His dad nodded, then said, 'Moving isn't so bad, you know.'

On the bookcase Arrietty had paused to look admiringly at some of Pete's action figures, which were exactly her size, but when she heard that, she froze. 'The beans are moving?' she said softly to herself.

Joe said, 'Maybe you'll like the new house even better. Try to keep an open mind.'

Pete sighed. 'OK,' he said bravely.

'Good.' His dad smiled rather sadly as he went out of the room.

On the bookshelf Arrietty was in a panic. 'This is big news,' she muttered. 'I have to tell the others!'

She spun round to run back, but accidentally bumped into an Indian figure. She tried to grab it, but it fell over the edge.

Pete looked up and, as Arrietty tried to slip back in among the toys, he yelled, 'Aha!' and tipped up his pencil holder.

He ducked round the side of the bookcase and peered carefully round the edge.

Arrietty didn't see him. Thinking she was safe, she slipped out – and found herself suddenly body-to-nose with a human boy's face. He had dark hair and dark eyes. The eyes were curious and the mouth had a friendly tilt to it. It was, all in all, a nice face, but so *huge*.

In his turn, Pete stared in total amazement at this tiny girl. She looked almost like some kind of doll, in her funny clothes made out of scrips and scraps, with a big button over her middle just like a baseball catcher's chest protector. Her pigtails looked like lollipops.

Arrietty screamed and tried to run, but Pete slammed the pencil holder down over her, slid a book under it and then lifted everything up so that he could look inside.

'Go ahead, bean,' Arrietty said defiantly.

'You can talk!' Pete exclaimed in delight.

'Of course I can. Now go on, get it over with.'

'Get what over with?' Pete asked.

'The squishing,' Arrietty said. 'You're going to squish me, aren't you?'

'Why do you want me to do that?'

'I don't want you to,' Arrietty explained, trying not to sound scared. 'It's what beans do.'

'Why do you keep calling me a bean?' Pete asked.

'Because that's what you are, a human bean.'

'I think you mean *being*,' Pete said, dropping her into an empty goldfish bowl. He tried to be careful, but she was so small and light she fell anyway, right on to her bottom.

'*Ouch!*' she yelled.

'Sorry,' Pete said quickly. 'I knew something was going on, but I never thought our stuff was being stolen by tiny people.'

'Stolen!' Arrietty was disgusted. 'We do not steal. We borrow. We are Borrowers, and you are our bean. You exist to provide us with things to borrow.'

'There are more of you?' Pete asked.

'My mother, Homily, my dad, Pod, and my brother, Peagreen.'

'We have to move,' Pete said sadly.

'I know,' Arrietty said. 'I heard. I hope the next family of beans is as untidy as you.'

'There won't be another family. The house belongs to this stupid man Potter, because my aunt who left us this house, forgot to write it in a will, and it's going to be torn down.'

'But what about us?' Arrietty asked. She was afraid all over again. 'This is terrible, really terrible!'

'Maybe there's some way I could help,' Pete said slowly.

SEVEN

ON SATURDAY, AS SOON as the big moving van drove away with all the heavy furniture, Pete was on the watch. A smaller van sat in the driveway, waiting for the last odds and ends.

When both his parents went back inside to check the empty house, Pete sneaked out, carefully carrying an ice-cream tub.

Inside was the Clock family, with as many of their belongings as they could carry.

Pod was saying nervously to Homily, 'I don't like putting the fate of my family into the hands of a trap-setting, Borrower-squishing ten-year-old bean. It goes against everything I was taught and believe in.'

'For once your father is right,' Homily replied, her arms crossed.

Arrietty didn't say anything. She knew they had no choice. Borrowers took weeks to move. Half that time would be spent in walking across the great, scary outside, trying to find another house to move to. Then they would have to work out how to move their things, and borrow what they needed to make the move. There had been no time for any of that – the beans had spent day and night in a whirlwind of packing, and the Clocks had stayed hidden lest they accidentally got squished by all the boxes and packages being stacked here and there or by busy bean feet walking back and forth.

Arrietty settled back and sighed. She knew her mother was worried about the new house. Would it be old enough for there to be spaces and places for Borrowers? Very new houses, Pod had said, were just like boxes, and Borrowers had trouble living in those. Arrietty groaned. She hated waiting. She wanted action.

Peagreen just nibbled on a tiny piece of chocolate, which he carried in both hands.

Meanwhile, Pete climbed into the back of the van, which jolted the poor Borrowers, making them and their belongings slide from side to side. He wedged them carefully between two boxes of books, then he pulled off the lid and looked down at the small, scared faces inside.

'We're in,' he said softly, and pointed to a toy walkie-talkie, which he'd strapped inside their container. 'With this I can let you know what's happening.'

'Listen up, bean,' Pod said fiercely. 'If anything happens to my family, I'm holding you personally responsible.'

'Yes, sir,' Pete said. He handed some sweets to Arrietty, but Peagreen jumped forward and grabbed them first. Then Pete pulled out Pod's stick and gave it to him. 'This must be yours.'

Pod took it, surprised and relieved to see it again. 'Why, thank you.'

From the house came the sound of Joe and Victoria's voices. 'That's the last of it,' Joe said.

Pete put the lid back on the ice-cream tub and helped his parents close up the back of the van, and then they all climbed in. Pete spoke softly into his walkie-talkie: 'We're just about to pull out. Over.'

Joe and Victoria exchanged looks. They

thought Pete was playing some kind of crazy game. This was better than his being depressed – they felt badly enough as it was.

'Well,' Joe said, 'I guess it's time to go.' He turned on the engine, and the van started to move.

Inside the ice-cream tub the family slid and jolted. Pete's voice came over the walkie-talkie: 'We're heading out of the drive. Over.'

Arrietty said to her nervous mother, 'Don't worry, everything will be fine.'

Peagreen held his stomach. 'Yeah, if you think throwing up is fun.'

Outside the tub, unseen by the Borrowers, the Lenders' belongings also slid about. An ironing board began to sway dangerously.

Inside the tub Pod said into the walkie-talkie, 'Bean, you're going too fast.' He backed away – then moved forward hastily. 'Over.'

In the van Pete said, 'Dad, could you slow down?'

Just then the tyres bumped over the kerb at the end of the driveway. The humans jolted in their seats. In the back the boxes jerked, and the ironing board came loose and smashed down

– cutting the ice-cream tub in half! Pod and Homily were thrown out on one side of the board, which now made a wall, and Arrietty and Peagreen on the other.

In the back seat Pete listened in terror to the screams and thumps coming from the Borrowers' walkie-talkie. 'Dad, you have to pull over!' he cried.

'What for?' Joe asked.

Pete hesitated. He loved his parents and wanted to tell them about the Borrowers, because he knew they'd never hurt the tiny people. But the only way he'd been able to convince Pod and Homily to let him help them had been to promise not to tell any other 'human beans' about the Borrowers – not even his parents.

So he said, 'I need to go the toilet.'

Victoria sighed. 'We just left the house!'

'I'm bursting!' Pete said desperately.

In the back of the van, Pod called to Peagreen and Arrietty to see if they were still alive.

Arrietty yelled, 'It's all right, Dad. We're OK.'

'I'll try to find a way around this thing,' Pod shouted.

But right then Joe braked in order to ease the back wheels off the kerb, which sent Arrietty and Peagreen sliding helplessly towards a hole in the floor of the van. They both tumbled through, holding on by their fingers and yelling for help.

'Dad,' Pete screamed, listening to his walkie-talkie. 'I feel sick! I smell gas! We've got to get out!'

Victoria sighed. 'Pete, cut it out.'

Joe manoeuvred the van forward just as Pod and Homily reached the hole where Arrietty and Peagreen were still dangling. It surged into motion.

Pete yelled wildly, 'Dad, it's my appendix. Stop, before it explodes!'

Joe shook his head. He thought that Pete was inventing excuses so they wouldn't have to move. 'Stop messing around,' he pleaded. 'You're just making this harder for us all.'

Joe started to drive faster – and in the back, Arrietty and Peagreen were knocked loose just before Pod could get to them. Both Borrower children fell into the street.

Arrietty straightened up, looking for her

brother. She spotted him standing in the middle of a nasty brown pile of dog poo.

Then she gasped.

The back wheels of the van were heading straight towards Peagreen!

EIGHT

POD PEERED THROUGH THE hole in the van floor, his heart pounding. He saw Peagreen duck down and the wheels whiz past him on either side. Peagreen was covered with mud and grass, but he was safe.

Pod leaned out further, just in time to see Arrietty and Peagreen pick themselves up and start walking back towards the house.

'Oh, Pod, what are we going to do?' Homily asked, near to tears. 'They don't know anything about the outside world. Why did you agree to this ridiculous idea in the first place?'

Pod put his arms around her. 'Me? I was agreeing with you. Besides, they're smart children. We have to trust them.'

He got up, frowning angrily. 'But if anything

does happen to them, the bean called Pete is going to pay.' He picked up a hairpin, which to Pod was as long as a sword, and he tested the tip for sharpness.

The van drove away up the street, taking poor Pod and Homily with it.

At the same moment, Arrietty and Peagreen saw a big, fancy car drive up in front of the house. As the Borrower children ran swiftly through the grass towards the house, they looked back and saw a huge man with a fancy moustache and in a fancy suit get out of the car.

His voice boomed across the lawn. 'Wait here, Wrigley. And if anyone comes, sound the horn.'

The bean inside the car said, 'Can I turn on the heating, Mr Potter? It's quite chilly.'

'No.' Mr Potter slammed the car door and walked up the front steps to the house. As he disappeared inside the Borrower children reached the foundations of the house.

They quickly made their way inside through the walls to their old living area under the floor. At once Arrietty began searching the walls, which were covered with old bits of paper –

including paper money, which to the Borrowers was just the same as any other paper.

'Ah! I knew it was here somewhere,' she said, pulling away a flyer from the wall. On the back was a street plan of the town. 'It's a map of the world,' Arrietty explained to Peagreen as she picked up the stub of an old eyebrow pencil and pointed to the flyer. 'Now. Here we are. And Pete said the new house is next to a church.'

Arrietty drew a line between the old house and the church. 'See? Not far at all.'

Peagreen snorted. 'Not far? Sure, if you're a giant. We were outside two minutes and look what happened to us. We fell three storeys, were nearly squished by a van and' – he sniffed at himself – 'and that wasn't mud. I'm covered in dog poo!'

Arrietty held her nose, then grinned. 'You don't get that kind of excitement every day, do you?'

Just then they heard noises in the house.

'*Shhh.* What's that?' Arrietty said. They ran down to a wall and peered through a crack.

Inside the front hallway Mr Potter finished nosing around. He set his briefcase down, opened it and took out a stethoscope, a blueprint and a hammer.

As he worked he said in a high voice, sounding like an old lady, '"I don't trust banks, Mr Potter, so I've hidden the will in the old house."' In his normal voice, he said nastily, 'Very wise, Mrs Alabaster, very wise.'

The Borrower children watched the lawyer get out the blueprint and orient himself. Then he began tapping at the walls with the hammer, listening carefully.

In the squeaky voice again he said, '"I have left the house to my niece Victoria, and enough money to keep the place up. You *will* make sure they get it, won't you, Mr Potter?"' And in his own voice, he gloated, 'You can trust *me*, Mrs Alabaster. I'm a lawyer!'

Just then a hollow sound came from the wall. Pleased, Mr Potter stopped tapping. He cleared away wallpaper and plaster to find a hidden safe and put on the stethoscope. Listing to the safe's tumblers, he slowly began turning the combination dial.

When the safe opened inside was an old metal box. Mr Potter opened the box and pulled out

Pod tightrope-walked across his rope and sat down on the counter to wipe his face. 'I'm getting too old for this,' he said.

'But we sat right here, in this office, when Aunt Mary said she was leaving the house to us! You were sitting right there!' said Joe Lender.

'Where there's no will,' Mr Potter said, his sympathy now so fake that even Joe noticed, 'there's no way.'

Arrietty started climbing up the refrigerator, which to someone her size was as large and scary as a big ice-white cliff.

The Borrowers watched their silverware and napkins fly up and stick to the ceiling as Victoria continued the vacuuming.

Mr Potter pulled an old metal box out of the safe. Inside was Mrs Alabaster's will.

'What kind of creepy-crawlies are we dealing with?' Jeff rubbed his hands.

Jeff swung the nozzle around. Thick white ooze splattered all over the lawyer's face. 'Youw!' Mr Potter screeched. 'Augh!'

Officer Steady walked up just then. 'Ah, I was hoping to see you,' he said cheerfully. 'I got you a tube of Dreamy Cream. For burns.'

Choking and coughing, Peagreen swam his way up to the top of the milk bottle.

Mr Potter was smashing every single milk bottle that came down the line.

Homily pulled the trigger. WHIZZ! The missile flew across the bottling room, trailing its string behind.

Three tons of slushy, mushy cottage cheese galloped right on to Mr Potter's head.

Potter flipped over a wire basket and imprisoned the Borrowers.

The Borrowers all lined up silently on every surface, some of them carrying handmade weapons. All waited together in silence.

'So,' Officer Steady said, 'little people, were they?' Mr Potter looked around fearfully. 'That's what I've been trying to tell you,' he said.

a folded sheet of paper. He unfolded it and held it up to the light – and Arrietty and Peagreen got a good look at the title.

THE LAST WILL AND TESTAMENT OF

MARY B. ALABASTER

'There *is* a will,' Arrietty whispered. 'That means we can save the house!'

Mr Potter still had the stethoscope to his ears. He frowned as if he'd heard voices – tiny voices, like those belonging to Borrowers. He looked around, and Arrietty and Peagreen jumped back, away from the hole in the wall.

When they peeked again more cautiously, they saw the lawyer take a cellular phone out of his briefcase. 'Potter here,' he said into the phone. 'It's twelve-thirty now. I'll be at the Town Hall to register the demolition. I want you to be ready by two. I want this house flattened *today*!'

Arrietty said, 'We've got to get that will to Pete!'

'Don't be stupid, Arrietty. How are we going to get it away from that huge bean?'

'I don't know,' she said, 'but we've got to try.'

Just then they saw Mr Potter hold the will up and strike at a fancy gold cigarette lighter. He was going to burn the will!

Click. Click! Click!

Impatiently the lawyer tried to get the lighter to work, but the spark would not ignite. In disgust he tossed the lighter away, dropped the will on to the mantelpiece, and started hunting round for matches.

'Come on,' Arrietty whispered, and she and Peagreen raced away.

Meanwhile, Mr Potter searched drawers and shelves for matches. But when he found some, he turned round – and stared.

The will was moving *all by itself* across the mantelpiece and on to some wall trim! Was it ghosts?

'What the . . .' he exclaimed, blinking his eyes, then rubbing them.

When the will reached a vent, he dropped down to grab it – but the will crumpled up and zipped through a hole, as if pulled by invisible fingers! Mr Potter yanked the stethoscope up to his ears and pressed it to the wall and now he distinctly heard little voices.

'Do you think he saw us?' Peagreen asked.

'No, I don't think so,' Arrietty replied.

Mr Potter went to the door and looked out. 'All right, who's there? Come on, show yourselves!'

No one appeared. Puzzled, the lawyer sniffed the air – then he made a face and checked his shoes. Something smelled suspiciously of dog poo, but he hadn't stepped in it. Somebody was in the house with him!

He got out the stethoscope again and this time listened at the floor, while underneath Arrietty and Peagreen were talking.

'Come on, squirt,' Arrietty was saying. 'We have to get this will out while the bean is on his lunch hour. That's always the safest time with beans.'

'I think we should wait for Mum and Dad,' Peagreen insisted.

'Peagreen, try to understand,' his big sister said firmly. 'There won't be a "here" unless we get this will to Pete before that nasty, cheating, thieving ugly bean destroys the house!'

Mr Potter frowned. 'Ugly?' he protested. 'Who are they calling ugly!'

He grabbed his hammer and used it to prise up the floor. Then he reached down and started feeling around.

Under the floor Arrietty and Peagreen were terrified when the roof of their old living area suddenly came free and a giant hand reached down. The poking, reaching fingers separated the two Borrower children.

'Come on, Peagreen!' Arrietty yelled as her brother pressed back against a wall.

But poor Peagreen couldn't get by that big, groping hand. The boy flattened himself as best he could. The thumb felt around, got closer, closer, then found his feet. It rose and poked him in the stomach and then in the face. The other fingers started to get closer.

'Arrietty . . .' Peagreen whispered.

Quick as a flash Arrietty pounced on an old fondue fork and jabbed it into the huge finger.

'*Yow!*' the lawyer yelled, and pulled his hand out.

Grabbing his hammer again, he pulled up more of the floorboard, and this time he stared down in total amazement. There in the flooring were tiny doorways and corridors, and tiny furniture – a house within the house! When he bent closer, he saw two tracks of tiny footsteps leading away from the area.

'Ugh,' he exclaimed. 'This house is infested!'

He pulled out his phone to call for reinforcements.

NINE

A VERY FEW MINUTES later, a truck screeched up outside the house. Mr Potter, who had been waiting impatiently, looked out. On the side of the truck was a sign that read: EXTERMINATOR JEFF THE PESTS' PEST.

Out of the truck bounded a nice young man, clean and spruce in his white exterminator's outfit.

He met Mr Potter at the front door. 'Greetings, how are you?'

Mr Potter made a sour face.

Exterminator Jeff said happily, 'It's nice to be doing business with you.'

'You're the only exterminator in the book,' Mr Potter said nastily.

Jeff was hurt and his smile disappeared. 'You said it was an emergency?'

'My house is infested.'

'What kind of creepy-crawlies are we dealing with?' Jeff rubbed his hands.

'That's your job. Now get to work,' Mr Potter ordered.

Jeff went out to get his equipment and came back with a sinister-looking fumigating tank covered with ominous warning labels. He strapped it on to his back, put some mean-looking goggles on his face and picked up the nozzle, which he held like a machine-gun.

Inside the walls, Arrietty and Peagreen hastily finished packing knapsacks with an old tape measure, a couple of pins – and the will.

Hearing noises in the front hall, Arrietty pushed up an old light-switch panel and peeked out from behind it. She took one look at Jeff in his exterminator's gear and her eyes went big and round.

'He's brought reinforcements. Quick!'

Just then Jeff looked down into the hole in the floor. He looked up in surprise. 'Borrowers!'

'You've seen them before?' Mr Potter demanded.

'No,' Jeff admitted. 'I thought they were just stories – you know, like the fly with the human head, poker-playing rats, giant radioactive roaches –'

'Can you kill them or not?'

'Why would you want to kill Borrowers?' Jeff looked unhappy.

'Those little rats stole something important from me, and no one steals from Ocious P. Potter!'

'Well, they're Borrowers, sir. They don't steal, they –' Jeff began.

Potter made a terrible face. 'Do your job! Or I'll make sure you never kill another bug in this town again. NOW!'

'Right,' Jeff said hastily.

He put the nozzle up to the Borrowers' former home and pulled the switch. Thick, white, nasty foam shot out, filling every open space.

Inside the floor Peagreen and Arrietty were busy trying to get away, but the foam was faster.

They looked back just in time to see a giant cloud of the stuff oozing along their path.

Jeff kept spraying until every nook and cranny of the Borrowers' old home was filled. 'Insecticide foam X-Tron B. Twelve bucks a can,' he said.

'What does it do?' Mr Potter demanded.

'Fills every bit of space and burns on contact. Awful stuff, actually.'

Mr Potter gave an evil grin. 'Burning?' he said. 'Burning's good.'

Down below, Arrietty and Peagreen scampered in fear, climbing through the walls as fast as they could. The foam bubbled after them, forcing them to go faster. Finally they popped out of a secret passage right on to the stair landing, the foam just behind them. As they watched, the foam hardened and stopped moving.

Back in the hallway Mr Potter waited impatiently. 'How long is this going to take?'

But Jeff was so busy with his job, he didn't hear. So Mr Potter tapped him on the shoulder

– and Jeff swung the nozzle round. Thick white ooze splattered all over the lawyer's face.

'*Youw!*' Mr Potter screeched. '*Augh!*'

Arrietty and Peagreen watched, laughing in relief.

Meanwhile, the foam had hardened in a cementlike mask over Mr Potter's face. Jeff pressed his foot against Mr Potter's chest and pulled and tugged at his face.

'Get it off me, you idiot!' Mr Potter howled. 'It burns!'

Jeff grunted, gave a mighty pull and the mask ripped free – and with it came Mr Potter's moustache, eyebrows, and a big chunk of his hair.

'My face!' the lawyer shouted. 'What have you done to my face?' He grabbed at his briefcase, took out a mirror and moaned as he looked at his red, hairless face. 'My moustache –'

He stopped. In the mirror he saw a strange sight – two little people, staring at him from the stair landing.

'Them!' At once Potter raced towards them, pausing to look back at Jeff. 'Now, get over here and help!'

But the Borrowers had disappeared again.

Mr Potter got his stethoscope and listened at the wall. A moment later he grinned, poking his pudgy finger at the wall. 'There!' he said.

Jeff whacked at the wall with the hammer's claw.

Inside the wall the gigantic claw of the hammer suddenly plunged through the plaster just inches away from Arrietty and Peagreen. They screamed and started to run.

Outside the wall Mr Potter kept pointing and yelling, 'There! There!'

Each time, Jeff smashed a big hole in the wall with his hammer, and each time, the hammer narrowly missed Arrietty and Peagreen.

Inside, the Borrower children reached a wooden wall support and froze, panting hard. Jeff went right on hammering, faster and faster, until he'd smashed a big hole in the wall. Then he stopped, also panting.

'Feel better?' Mr Potter asked with a sour smile.

Jeff nodded, grinning sheepishly.

Mr Potter bent close to the wall with his stethoscope. Arrietty pulled a paper clip from her pack and tossed it away as far as she could.

Clink! It landed well away from the Borrowers. Mr Potter heard it and frowned. Quietly he moved to another hole and sniffed. *Ugh!* Dog poo!

With an evil smile, Mr Potter tapped the wall right outside where the Borrowers stood and he motioned to Jeff. The hammer smashed through the wall – and the claw caught Peagreen's jacket, pulling him out of the new hole.

'Arrietty!' Peagreen wailed.

Jeff lifted the hammer for another smash and Peagreen flew into the air.

TEN

POOR PEAGREEN SAILED UP and up and *up*. He bumped into a dangling light bulb and grabbed on as tight as he could. The floor below looked a hundred miles away.

Mr Potter looked up, saw him – and started jumping up towards the ceiling, trying to grab the Borrower boy off the light bulb.

Back in the wall, Arrietty watched in horror. Then she got an idea. She peered out, ducked back and vanished.

'Do something, do something!' the lawyer yelled at Jeff.

Exterminator Jeff pointed at the light switch. Mr Potter gave his sinister smile. 'I like the way you think.'

Jeff flicked the light on and Peagreen felt the glass under his body start getting hot. Below him he saw the horrible Potter bean position himself with his hands cupped. He was waiting for Peagreen to fall.

Peagreen knew that Pete had been safe – he would never squish Borrowers. This Potter bean, however, was definitely a squisher. '*Ow, ow, ow,*' he cried. 'It hurts.'

The bulb just got hotter. Desperately Peagreen looked around for some kind of escape. Anything was better than being squished – except being fried to a crisp. He looked round, and down, and up. In surprise and delight, he saw Arrietty poke her head out from a hole in the ceiling where the light bulb's cord came out.

'Grab hold!' she ordered. And she quickly lowered the tape measure from her pack.

Below, Mr Potter growled in anger. He snatched the hammer away from Jeff and lunged towards the ceiling, hoping to smash the light bulb – and the Borrower boy with it. But just as the hammer was whizzing through the air towards the light bulb, Peagreen grabbed the tape measure. Arrietty pressed the button on the side of the measure and – *zzziiip!* – Peagreen whizzed up into the ceiling.

The hammer smashed into the light, sending glass flying everywhere, and the claw stuck on the wires – sending big volts of electricity right down the hammer to Mr Potter.

'*Whoo-ooo-ooo!*' The lawyer wiggled and jumped as electricity zapped through him.

A tiny jacket had got stuck to the hammer. Jeff was so interested in looking at it that he forgot about Mr Potter.

'*T*–t–urm . . . ogh . . . d–d–uh . . . erec-tricery!' Mr Potter stuttered.

'Huh?' Jeff said. He looked up and started in surprise when he saw Mr Potter with smoke coming out of his ears, his hair standing straight up. 'Oh!'

He hit the light switch and Mr Potter thudded to the floor.

Then the hammer fell off the light bulb and conked him on the head.

Meanwhile, Arrietty and Peagreen climbed out on to the roof. There, they looked in amazement at the big blue sky and the rooftops of the town stretching away to the horizon.

'It's the world,' Arrietty said, scared and delighted at once.

'Wow,' Peagreen said in awe.

'I never thought there'd *be* so much world in the whole wide world!' Arrietty exclaimed, suddenly longing to explore it all at once.

But first they had to escape, and Peagreen was her responsibility.

She took her brother's hand and they made their way carefully over the jumble of stuff on the roof until they reached the edge. Arrietty stood silently, looking at the phone wires stretching out to the poles and then from pole to pole all the way down the street. In the distance she could see the spire of the church. 'We've got to make for that if we want to find them,' she said, pointing.

'Can't we just stay here?' Peagreen said.

'If we stay here we'll be squished for sure.'

'But if we go out there?'

Arrietty said, 'We only *might* get squished. Now look at these wires. That's how we have to get down.'

Frightened, Peagreen looked out at the phone wires, then back at his grinning sister. 'I hate you, Arrietty Clock,' he said.

ELEVEN

RIGHT ABOUT THE SAME time that Arrietty and Peagreen climbed up on to the roof, Pete and his parents pulled up in front of their new house. It was small and plain and very, very modern. Pete hated it on sight. He looked at his parents and he could tell from their faces that they hated it too.

'Here we are – home,' Joe said, trying to be cheerful.

Victoria wiped her eyes, then smiled bravely.

Pete jumped out of the back seat and ran round to the van's back doors.

Victoria called, 'Don't you want to see the house?'

'No,' Pete said. 'I have to check my stuff.'

Despite the awful situation, Joe grinned and

teased, 'I thought you needed immediate medical attention!'

Pete gave his dad a desperate smile. 'I'm feeling a lot better.'

His parents went inside the new house to decide where to put things. When they were safely out of sight, Pete opened the back of the van. Shock ran through him when he saw the ruined ice-cream tub. He started searching desperately for the Borrowers.

Pod and Homily crept cautiously out from behind a box, and Pete exclaimed in relief, 'You're all right! But where are Arrietty and Peagreen?'

'They fell through,' Homily said, her face wet with tears. 'They're lost!'

Pod said angrily, 'We trusted you, bean. From now on, *I'm* calling the shots. Got it?'

Pete nodded, and a few minutes later he wheeled his bicycle down the ramp of the big furniture van. Following Pod's instructions he'd used duct tape to secure a coffee can to the handlebars.

He lifted the lid of the can. 'Where to, Mr Clock?'

Inside, the Borrower parents looked up at him. 'Back to the old house – pronto!'

Just then Victoria came out of the front door of the new house. 'Pete, where are you going?'

'Nowhere, Mum,' Pete shouted over his shoulder, pedalling as fast as he could, before his parents could stop him.

Inside the can Pod held Homily's hand. 'Did I ever tell you,' he said, 'about the time Minty got jammed in the cookie jar?'

Meanwhile, back at the old house, Mr Potter was very, very angry. 'I must look ridiculous,' he snapped.

Jeff took a glance at his expensive suit, now flecked with nasty dried foam and burned from the jolt of electricity. He looked at Mr Potter's round face, all red and sweaty and hairless, with his moustache and part of his eyebrows missing. His hair stood up like a fright wig and foam bits speckled it. Jeff looked away and said, 'You look fine.'

Mr Potter, enraged, snarled, 'This is all your fault! Now I look like a freak!'

'No, sir,' Jeff said, trying to calm him down. 'You're still a very handsome man.'

'Oh, shut up,' the angry lawyer said. 'Now find those Borrowers or you're in big trouble!'

Jeff said, 'Then I believe it's time to introduce my secret weapon.' He raced out and returned a minute later leading a lazy brown dog with droopy ears and a wrinkly face. 'Say hello to Mr Smelly.'

Mr Potter looked down in disgust at the dog, who sat down and scratched himself with a hind leg. '*That's* your secret weapon?'

'You're probably wondering how he got his name,' Jeff said.

Just then the dog let loose a long, loud fart.

'No, I wasn't,' Mr Potter said, making a sour face.

Mr Smelly gave another blast, even longer and louder than the first one. Mr Potter started waving his hands to get the smell away. 'That's awful. What do you feed that animal?'

'Cheese,' Jeff said. He held out the charred little coat, which had fallen off when Peagreen had climbed up the measuring tape. 'Here, boy. Scent!'

The dog sniffed at the coat, then lifted his head, suddenly alert. Jeff struggled to hold the leash tight as the dog led the two men down to the front garden – where, to their surprise, a policeman had just arrived.

They both knew Officer Steady, the town constable.

'Good morning, gentlemen. Fine day, isn't it?' Officer Steady was always courteous and friendly. He peered at the lawyer, looking concerned. 'What happened to your face?'

Potter clenched his teeth in impatience. 'What is it, officer?'

'A slight disturbance of the peace has been reported,' Officer Steady said. 'Two men – would that be you, sirs? – were reported coming into this house. Shortly thereafter, disturbing noises were heard emanating from same.'

'It's my house,' Mr Potter said. 'I can do what I want.'

'Is it, sir? I thought it belonged to the Lenders. Such a nice family.'

'It belongs to me now,' Mr Potter roared, 'so bug off!'

'Not really a polite way to talk to an officer

of the law, is it, sir?' Officer Steady said calmly. 'Courtesy is the glue that holds society together.'

Furious, the lawyer put his face close to the policeman's, as though to scare him off. But Officer Steady only said, 'You should really put some cream on that skin.'

Potter turned away in disgust and stomped down the street and round the corner, Jeff and Mr Smelly trailing along behind. The officer went off the other way.

At that moment Pete rose up, his bike skidding. He took one look at the exterminator truck in the driveway and gasped.

'Oh, no!'

TWELVE

MOMENTS LATER PETE AND the Borrower parents stood inside the old house, looking around at the mess. Most of the foam had dried up into dust, but there was still some left in corners and cracks.

Homily's eyes were big and tear-filled. 'Oh, Pod,' she said, clutching her husband. 'The children . . .'

Pete looked down at them, sitting on top of the coffee can, which he held carefully in his hands. Then he looked up again, hoping he'd find some sign of Arrietty and Peagreen.

But it was Pod who spotted their first clue.

Motioning to Pete to put him down near their old living area, he spied the map that Arrietty had peeled off the wall. Then, tracing the line that she'd drawn from the old house to the church, Pod grinned. 'It's all right,' he said happily. 'They're not here. Look. They're going to the new house.' He pointed to the map. 'Clever girl!'

'Thank heavens,' Homily said, clasping her hands. 'For a moment I thought – well, I can hardly bear to think of what I thought!'

Pete said, 'Try not to worry, Mrs Clock. I'm sure everything will be just fine.'

Homily looked up at the huge bean. 'Fine?' She sniffed, pointing around the room. 'Look at it, just look at what they've done to our lovely home. It's as though someone's gone insane with fury.'

Pod grinned. 'Arrietty does have that effect on people.'

'True,' Arrietty's mother said. 'But even so, what kind of maniac would do something like this?'

Pete nodded in agreement, looking around at the mess of dried foam and the huge holes in the walls. Glass crunched underfoot from a mangled light bulb.

Then he saw something golden, glinting in the

mess by the stairway. Walking over, he picked it up. It was a gold lighter, engraved with the name *O. Potter, Esq.* Pete held up the lighter for the Borrowers to see.

'This kind,' he said.

At that moment up on the roof, Arrietty had just finished putting together all the things she had borrowed. She'd found two clothes pegs, and together she and Peagreen had made a vehicle out of each. They hooked them over the wires, held on – and jumped off the edge of the roof.

Whizzzz! They swooped down the phone lines to the telephone pole.

'*Wheeeee!*' Arrietty yelled. She loved it!

'*Yoooooowwww!*' Peagreen followed her, feeling like he'd left his stomach back up on the roof and it wasn't any too happy.

Whizzzz! They reached the roof gutter of the next house and Arrietty helped the shaky Peagreen climb down from his clothes peg.

'Fun, isn't it?' she asked.

'You must be missing part of your brain,' Peagreen muttered.

'I know,' Arrietty said, with big-sister superiority. 'Otherwise I wouldn't spend so much time with a little squirt like you.'

Upholding the rights of little brothers everywhere, Peagreen forgot his terror and fired back, 'Who are you calling a squirt, bean-face?'

'Who are you calling bean-face, stupid?'

Peagreen was about to answer when they heard noises coming from the street below them. Both children were silent now as they cautiously took a look.

They were just in time to see Mr Potter, Jeff and Mr Smelly arrive. Then, as the Borrowers watched, the dog sniffed the air, looked up and began to bark, jumping up towards them.

Arrietty and Peagreen flattened themselves against the roof shingles at their backs, not even daring to breathe.

From below came Jeff's voice: 'Best nose in town. *Shhh!*'

Peagreen edged his foot to the left, trying to make himself even flatter. But then he became aware that he was not alone. He turned his head – and looked right into the eye of a huge pigeon.

He screamed and jumped away, losing his balance.

For a second his arms windmilled desperately. Arrietty reached for him, but he overbalanced and plopped into the rain gutter, rolling towards the drainpipe.

'*Yaaaaaaugh!*' he wailed as he shot down the pipe.

Ploink! He popped out of the end and landed in an empty glass milk bottle, spinning dizzily as the bottle teetered round and round from the impact.

Mr Potter, Jeff and the dog heard the tinkling sound of the milk bottle spinning, and the lawyer yelled in triumph, 'Got one!'

All three of them started towards the bottle, with Peagreen helpless inside. But before they could reach it, Mr Potter looked up and down the street, then he scowled.

Officer Steady walked up just then. 'Ah, I was hoping to see you,' he said cheerfully. 'I've got you a tube of Dreamy Cream. For burns.'

Up above, Arrietty was relieved to see Mr Potter and Jeff's attention turn to the constable. Quickly she tied her dental floss rope into a brace, then began lowering herself down the pipe.

Meanwhile, Mr Potter was not grateful for the tube of cream. In fact, he was desperate, for just then a milkman drove up, parked, and started heading for the milk bottles – including the one with Peagreen in it.

Mr Potter eyed the friendly constable. Yes, he'd be just the type for stopping a desperate lawyer from squishing some deserving Borrowers. Hoping to get rid of the officer, he snarled, 'Don't you have anything better to do? Like fight crime?'

Officer Steady was not going to be chased away by bad manners. In fact, he just got more cheerful. 'Crime is but one small slice of the policing pie, sir,' he said. 'I'm a great believer in simple, personal – dare I say it? – intimate service. There, I've said it. After all, you can only put out one fire at a time.' He smiled hopefully, with the air of a constable who was willing to wait all day for Mr Potter to cheer up.

The lawyer sneaked another glance towards the milkman. He had to get to those bottles first! 'You know,' he said with a big, fake smile, 'I could listen to you all day, but I really have to go!'

Officer Steady still stood in his way. 'Sorry to hear that,' the constable said politely. 'I've quite enjoyed talking with you as well. Good day, sir. And good luck with your face.'

Arrietty reached the bottom of the drainpipe just then, but she and Mr Potter and Jeff watched helplessly as the milkman put Pea-green's bottle into the back of his truck with the others. A moment later he drove away.

Mr Potter, Jeff and Mr Smelly ran after the milkman – watched by Pete, who had just come out of the house.

Inside the coffee can Homily said, 'What is it, Pete? Why have we stopped?'

Pete pulled the lid off the can. 'It's odd. Mr Potter, the other man and a big, drooly dog have just started chasing a milkman.'

'Do you think . . . ?' Homily said to Pod.

'What else could it be?' Pod said back, and to Pete, 'Come on, bean, follow that bean!'

THIRTEEN

PETE COULDN'T SEE ARRIETTY, who was hiding by the drainpipe, and her parents were now inside the coffee can, so they couldn't see her either. Poor Arrietty was completely alone – and worse, she'd run out of ideas.

She sat on the kerb, her feet dangling over the gutter. Her eyes filled with tears and she wiped them on her sleeve.

A voice spoke from below. 'What's the matter now?'

Arrietty jumped and looked around wildly. 'Who said that?'

A Borrower boy climbed out of the gutter and stood looking down at her. She stared back, amazed. The boy was about her age, kind of wild-looking, dressed stylishly in clothes made out of scraps and litter.

'You're a Borrower!' she exclaimed.

'Nothing wrong with your eyesight then,' the boy said, grinning.

'I really didn't believe there were any more of us left,' Arrietty said.

'Well, here I am, living proof. My name is Spiller. Spud Spiller.'

Arrietty was still surprised, but she remembered her manners. 'Arrietty Clock,' she said, offering her hand.

Spiller shook it. 'Ah,' he said. 'You're an innie. That explains it.'

'An "innie"?' she repeated.

'You know. A house Borrower. Someone who depends on beans for a living.'

Arrietty was annoyed. 'I don't depend on anyone, thank you very much. Now, if you'll excuse me, I have to find my brother.'

'They've taken him to the dairy,' Spiller said. 'You can try walking all the way there if you like, but I wouldn't recommend it.'

'Have you got a better idea?'

'I've got a faster one,' Spiller said, giving her

a challenging grin. 'Come on.' He held out his hand.

Reluctantly Arrietty took it and he helped her climb down the gutter. Inside, which was dark and smelt of mud and damp, mouldy rubbish, Spiller led the way to a round tunnel. 'This used to be the old water pipe,' he explained, his voice echoing weirdly. 'Now . . . it's the Spiller Expressway! And this –'

He struck a match and the area filled with light. Arrietty's mouth dropped open. Before her was an aerosol can fitted on to a roller skate.

'– is the Spiller Express,' the boy said. 'Don't worry, innie, it's perfectly safe.'

'I'm not worried,' Arrietty said promptly. 'And I wish you'd stop calling me that.'

'It's what you are, isn't it?'

'Well, if I'm an innie,' she said, following him on to the Spiller Express, 'what does that make you, an "outie"?'

'Of course,' he said, reaching for another match. 'My roof is the open sky, my floor the green grass, my walls are the tall trees. Well,' he added, handing her a helmet made out of a walnut shell, 'if you want to be a hundred per cent accurate, my walls are the shed next to the compost heap.' He strapped on his own helmet. 'Now remember, safety first.'

Arrietty snorted. 'If I'd put safety first I wouldn't have got into this contraption in the first place.'

Spiller grinned, lit the match and touched it to a waiting candle. Then he reached for the handbrake, which was made from a safety pin. He pressed the button that started the aerosol spray and a second later the car shot down the pipe like a spacecraft in flight.

Spiller glanced at Arrietty. If he had expected her to be scared, he was disappointed, for she was grinning in delight. This girl liked speed!

The Spiller Express swooped down and up and around, guided by Spiller, who knew where every building was in the town. So he and Arrietty arrived at the dairy just about the same time the milk truck with Peagreen's bottle pulled in.

Poor Peagreen, meanwhile, tried to keep up his courage by singing. The only song he seemed to be able to think of, though, was 'Ninety-nine bottles of milk hanging on the wall, ninety-nine bottles of milk . . .'

The milkman started unloading milk bottles on to a cart. Peagreen's bottle was in the middle of a big jumble and the milkman didn't see him.

Peagreen peered through the glass, which made things look even bigger and scarier and weirder than they did already. Then something jolted slightly and his bottle started moving.

The bottles passed through a flap and into a vast room with lots of huge machines. Peagreen kept singing.

At the other end of the dairy, Spiller pulled on the brake and the Express screeched to a halt in a shower of sparks.

'Well, what do you think?' he asked Arrietty, pulling off his helmet.

'Is that as f-fast as you can g-go?' she asked bouncing up and down.

Spiller laughed and led the way up the pipe into the dairy. 'What are a couple of nice Borrowers like you and your brother doing outside anyway?' he asked as they climbed.

'We were emigrating to a new house,' she explained in a quick voice. 'We were in an ice-cream tub and it got chopped in two by an ironing board, and we fell through the floor of the van and my brother nearly got squished, then we walked for ever back to the house, where these horrible beans tried to kill us with foam and hammers and so we got on to the roof and slid down and were trying to find our way back to our parents when this dog –'

Spiller pounced on the words that surprised him the most. 'You have *parents*?'

'Of course. Doesn't everyone?' she replied.

Spiller pushed up a grate and Arrietty stared in amazement at the huge room full of tall, complicated machines and conveyor belts criss-crossing this way and that. 'I've never seen anything like this,' she murmured.

'It's an automated bottling plant,' Spiller said. 'They bring in empties, wash, dry, fill and cap them, then send them out again. It's a great place to come if you like speed, excitement and as much milk as you can drink.'

'Poor Peagreen,' Arrietty said, looking around. 'He hates milk.'

'Don't worry. I know this place. We'll find him –'

Spiller stopped. In the distance, very faintly,

they could hear a high voice – a Borrower voice.

'And if one milk bottle should accidentally fall . . .'

'That's Peagreen,' Arrietty exclaimed.

They spotted his bottle heading down an automated bottle run, right towards the washer. They started to run.

'See?' Spiller said. 'Found him in no time!'

'Spiller!'

'Keep your hair on,' Spiller said. 'From what I saw, he could do with a bath. Anyway, I've got a plan.'

While he and Arrietty kept running, poor Peagreen was moving slowly towards a giant machine that made a horrific racket and had steam billowing out of the sides. He tried jumping up and down in a futile attempt to escape, but his bottle was carried inside the dark mouth of the machine.

Soapy water rained down on him. Peagreen scrunched down into the bottle, holding his hands over his head. He emerged from the machine waist-deep in soapy water, and was promptly doused with clear water. When he emerged from that, his hair was plastered down, his clothes were soggy and water still sloshed around in his bottle.

Blinking water out of his eyes, he looked ahead – just as mechanical grippers seized his bottle and turned it upside-down over a long drop, with a hard cement floor below. Peagreen almost fell out, but he threw out his arms and legs and managed to keep himself wedged inside.

Then Peagreen gulped in terror. Ahead was a red-hot, glowing drying machine. And he was being carried right to it.

FOURTEEN

Mr Potter was furious. He did not like having to run through the streets with his face burned, his hair standing on end and his clothes messy. Even worse was having to run behind what had to be the gassiest, stinkiest dog in the world.

But the dog, Jeff and Mr Potter finally arrived outside the dairy and hustled round to the front door. Unseen by them, Pete skidded his bike to a stop. He watched as they disappeared inside the front door, then grabbed up the coffee can and followed them. When he got to the door, he heard it lock from the inside.

Inside, Arrietty and Spiller clambered up riveting struts, each holding on to either end of a paper towel, unfurling it from a nearby roll as they climbed.

'Spiller?' Arrietty asked. 'Have you really not got any parents?'

'Well,' he said nonchalantly, 'I didn't hatch out of an egg, if that's what you mean. But I didn't know them. Grew up with my Uncle Root. Everyone called him Sparrow, on account of he was so big.'

'Where is he now?' Arrietty asked as they kept working.

'Killed by a cat. Everyone always told him it was a ridiculous animal for a Borrower to keep as a pet.'

As they talked they gathered up the end of the paper towel and tied it off so that it stretched under the bottle carrier. Then they knotted the towel on the other side to make it secure.

Just in time – they saw Peagreen coming towards them.

Peagreen saw them as well. 'Arrietty!' he yelled.

'You're going to have to jump,' Arrietty called.

'Oh noooo,' Peagreen moaned, looking down

at the paper towel 'net' below. It looked terribly small and the drop really long. But it was better than the heat machine.

He slipped through the bottle-neck and fell with a splat on to the paper net. Spiller and Arrietty braced it – and Peagreen bounced once and was safe.

He sat up. 'I'm hungry,' he said. 'Who's that?'

'I'm Spiller,' said the new Borrower. 'But you can call me Spud. Who're you?'

Unnoticed, Peagreen's wet bottom had made a hole in the paper towel. 'Hi, Spud. I'm Peagreeeeeeeeen!' he wailed, falling through – right into another bottle. 'I hate this place!' he cried.

Spiller and Arrietty watched the bottle being carried towards the milker – then she turned to Spiller and said, 'What now, genius?'

Spiller grabbed Arrietty and leapt on to a row of upside-down bottles that were moving alongside Peagreen. Then he uncoiled a rope from around his waist, whirled it round his head and threw it. Bull's-eye! It hit the edge of Peagreen's bottle and fell down inside.

Peagreen reached up to grab it, but then the

rope vanished as his bottle took a hard right turn. He looked up and the milk nozzle loomed closer, closer, then squirted a waterfall of milk on to him.

Choking and coughing, Peagreen swam his way up to the top, but before he could climb out – *wham! snap!* – another machine slammed a cap on to the bottle, which was then secured by another machine.

From a window Pete, Pod and Homily were watching. All three were horrified.

Pod pointed frantically at the bottom of the door. 'Pete, put us there!'

Pete grabbed the coffee can and set it down. He couldn't get inside the locked door, but the Borrowers could slip under it.

A sudden noise at the other end of the room made everyone look up. Mr Potter had gone to the conveyor belt that carried the upside-down empty bottles and he was smashing with a monkey wrench every single one that came down the line. Arrietty and Spiller took one look at that fierce face and the flying glass, and they started to run backwards along their row of bottles. Spiller stumbled and almost fell, catching hold of the edge of a bottle bottom with one hand. Arrietty reached down to pull him up.

Meanwhile, Pod and Homily ran in and saw Peagreen in his bottle. Pod started working like a maniac, busily making a ballpoint pen and rubber bands into a shoulder-held rocket launcher.

Homily put the missile together, her hands blurring with speed as she secured a pin to a matchstick with thread. 'Pod,' she said, 'if we all get out of this alive, I'll never complain again about your tracking mud on our carpet.'

'Oh, good,' Pod said, grunting with effort as he stretched the rubber band.

'You know what else?' Homily said, trying to sound calm as she finished tying off the thread. 'I don't even care if we never have another carpet.'

'Ready?' Pod asked.

'Ready.' Homily nodded.

Pod shouldered the launcher and Homily loaded in her missile, pushing it hard against the rubber band. Pod lifted the launcher and squinted down its length to aim. 'I'm getting too old for this,' he muttered.

'Here,' Homily said, holding out her hand.

Pod said, 'Have you ever shot one of these before?'

'You're not the only one with a past,' she said, taking aim.

Zing! She pulled the trigger. *Whizzz!* The missile flew across the bottling room, trailing its string behind. *Bink!* It hit right on target, spearing the top of Peagreen's bottle.

Homily then held on to one end of the line as Pod whooshed down it, hanging on to a paper clip. Just as, inside the bottle, poor Peagreen ran out of air and went down for the last time, Pod smacked into the bottle, knocking it out of the line. He rode piggyback on the bottle neck as it plunged down and then smashed on to the floor.

Pod rolled off and tumbled to a stop. Digging through the huge shards of glass, he waded through the lake of milk until he found Peagreen, who was lying very still in the middle of the mess.

'Don't give up on me, son,' Pod said, pushing on his chest.

Peagreen gave a cough and opened his eyes. 'I hate milk,' he croaked.

Behind them Mr Potter was still smashing glasses. 'It's the end of the line, vermin!' he yelled.

Meanwhile, Arrietty managed to pull Spiller back up on to the milk bottles. At once the Borrower boy pointed out a platform near a lot of switches. Then he took careful aim and threw his lasso so that it caught on a lever. He pulled the rope tight, yanked it down and both he and Arrietty held on to it, swooping down.

Zoink! zoink! zoink!

A warning siren went off and Mr Potter looked around in surprise.

'Say cheese,' Spiller yelled.

Mr Potter looked up – just as a giant chute opened up right above him.

Three tons of slushy, mushy cottage cheese galloped right on to his head. He staggered, yelling angrily, then fell in the wave of glop. Arrietty and Spiller clutched their sides, laughing hard. The Potter bean had rolled into the trough built to hold all that cheese and got stuck at the end.

The bottle carrier ran right past his face, so that the bottles now started hitting him on the head. *Plink! Plonk! Clonk!* Spiller and Arrietty laughed even harder. Vermin? They'd show *him*!

'Cheese!' the furious lawyer howled.

Snorfling noises came from below as Mr Smelly started gobbling up his favourite food. PH-H-H-HT! He let out a mighty blast right at the lawyer.

'Jeff!' Mr Potter yelled.

The exterminator leapt to help his uncle.

On the other side of the room, Arrietty and Spiller, still laughing, reached her parents and brother. Pod and Homily hugged both of their children. Spiller faded back.

Finally Pod noticed Spiller standing by awkwardly. 'Who is this?'

'This is Spiller,' Arrietty said, smiling. 'He helped us out.'

Pod offered his hand. Spiller reached forward with a fist. Then, to his family's surprise, Pod made a fist and bopped Spiller's hand. Spiller bopped back, but he was as surprised as the Clocks.

He turned to Arrietty. 'Why didn't you tell me your father was an outie?'

'He is?' Arrietty said, and turned to her father. 'You are?'

Pod smiled at her. 'I was. That was before I met your mother.'

A long shadow fell over them, preventing any more talk.

The Borrowers looked up – to find a cheesy, burn-faced, ANGRY Mr Potter. He had a broom and dustpan in his hands. 'My, my,' he said nastily. 'The whole thieving family, together at last! I'll take *that*,' he said, grabbing the folded will from Arrietty's backpack.

The Borrowers started to run.

'And I'll take *this*,' he gloated, reaching down with the broom.

And with one mighty sweep, he captured them all in the dustpan.

FIFTEEN

WITHIN MINUTES THE VILLAINOUS lawyer had all five Borrowers taped flat right in the middle of the big cheese pan. They all fought and wiggled desperately, but the clear tape the lawyer had used made it impossible for them to budge.

Mr Potter stood at the control panel, growling and muttering to himself as he punched buttons and threw switches. Exterminator Jeff stood by waiting as Potter finished and then – with an evil grin – hit a large red button labelled CHEESE FILL.

The Borrowers heard one of the big machines hum to life. Overhead, inside a big steel vat, ominous noises began. *Glorp! Blurp!* The needle on a big dial, with the word FULL at the top, began to rise slowly.

Mr Potter reached for the final switch, but just before his fingers touched it, Spiller yelled, 'Hey, pizza-face!'

The lawyer whirled around.

'Yeah, over here, you great monstrosity!'

Worried, Arrietty whispered, 'What are you doing?'

Mr Potter loomed over the cheese pan. 'Are you talking to me, you poisonous little rodent?' he snarled.

'Yeah,' Spiller said, his eyes narrowed. 'I'm talking to you, fatso. Just because you're bigger, you think you can do what you like.'

Mr Potter laughed nastily. 'As a matter of fact, I do.'

'Yeah. I'll bet you can't get a girlfriend, not with a pizza for a face!'

The lawyer glowered. 'You know, I'm thinking that perhaps being slowly suffocated by two tons of low-fat dairy-cheese whip is too good for you.'

Spiller taunted, 'Yeah? And what are you going to do, grind me in the waste pipe?'

Mr Potter glanced over at a big pipe labelled SOLID WASTE. He smiled. 'Hmmm. Interesting idea.'

Spiller said quickly, 'I was just joking. Sorry.' He started to struggle. 'Please, not the waste pipe. Anything but that!'

Laughing, the lawyer untaped Spiller, picked him up and carried him over to the pipe. He held him up. 'Any last words?'

'You know,' Spiller said, brave to the last, 'you really should put some cream on that face. You look disgusting.'

Mr Potter angrily tossed him inside the pipe, then slammed the switch. The pipe immediately made horrible grinding noises.

'Nooo!' Arrietty screamed.

Mr Potter stomped back to the master control panel and this time he threw the final switch. Then he returned to the cheese pan.

'I'd love to stay and watch,' he said, 'but I have a date with destruction!' He started to leave, pushing his way past Jeff and Mr Smelly.

Jeff followed, but he looked back doubtfully at the Borrowers, who were still fighting to get free of the tape. On the dial the needle slowly climbed towards FULL. And next to the FULL sign was a light for CHEESE RELEASE.

'You're not going to just leave them there, are you?' Jeff asked him.

The lawyer ignored him and stamped out of the door.

Outside, Pete ran into Mr Potter. 'Wait! What have you done with my friends?'

'Get over it,' the angry lawyer snarled, pushing the boy out of his way. 'Find some kids your own size.'

In desperation Pete cried, 'Wait! You can't do this!' He grabbed Mr Potter's suit coat and – *rrrripp!* – the fabric tore.

'You wanna know what happened to your pals?' Mr Potter said fiercely, shoving him away. 'They're about to be *cheesed*!' He jumped into his car and slammed the door. Then he rolled down his window and yelled to Jeff, 'Are you coming?'

Pete didn't wait to hear the answer. He had to get inside and save his friends.

Mr Potter yelled at his chauffeur to drive on. The big limo backed up – and knocked down Pete's bike, crunching it under the wheels. Then it pulled forward and smashed the bike a second time.

Inside the car Mr Potter held up the will and reached for his lighter. He patted all his pockets, then remembered that he'd left it at the house. 'Town Hall, Wrigley,' he commanded. 'Chop-chop!'

'Certainly, sir,' the chauffeur said. 'Would that be observing or not observing the local speed limit?'

'Just drive, you moron!'

Meanwhile, Pete had looked all over for some way to get in. Just as he was about to give up, a milk truck pulled away from the wall, revealing a loading chute. Grinning, Pete lunged towards it and crawled inside through the chute.

He looked around desperately, trying to work out which machine made cheese. He couldn't see the Borrowers anywhere.

Back in the cheese pan, Pod said, 'Don't lose hope, Arrietty. If there's one thing we outies know, it's how to survive.'

They all looked up at the dial, which was

steadily moving towards the FULL limit. When it reached FULL, they knew the cheese would come pouring down.

Pete spotted the machine – and he saw the dial nearly at FULL. Ten seconds to go! Nine . . .

He climbed up on to the bottle washer and leapt to the dryer.

Three . . . two . . .

Pete vaulted desperately across the equipment.

Voink! Voink! Voink! Red flashing lights went off. The light next to CHEESE RELEASE came to life.

Below the nozzle the Borrowers wriggled desperately. Nearby Pete made a last leap, grabbed on to the cheese nozzle and shoved it out of the way. The effort made him lose his balance and he fell flat on his back, with the nozzle right above him!

He rolled away just as a huge, yellow-orange blob of gunk came out of the nozzle. *Splat!* A ton of cheese slammed on to the floor where Pete had been a moment before.

He hopped to his feet and raced to the cheese pan.

Pod grinned at him. 'I never thought I'd say these words, bean, but I'm glad to see you.'

Pete grinned back as he reached down to remove the tape from the Borrowers. As he worked Arrietty said anxiously, 'Pete, that Potter has the will and he's heading for the Town Hall. If you hurry, you can save our home!'

'Me? What about you?' Pete asked.

'Don't worry,' Arrietty said. 'We'll meet you there.'

Pete ran outside.

Led by Arrietty, the Borrowers ran to a grate in the floor.

Behind them, leading away from the waste pipe, were tiny footprints.

SIXTEEN

PETE SKIDDED TO A halt, his mouth open in dismay, when he saw his crushed bike. But before he could say anything, a truck honked behind him.

He looked up. There was Exterminator Jeff, smiling out the driver's window. 'Need a lift?' he asked.

Pete grinned and hopped inside.

'Where are the Borrowers?' Jeff asked as he raced out of the dairy parking lot.

'They're going to meet us at the Town Hall,' Pete said.

'How are they going to get there?' Exterminator Jeff asked.

Down in the tunnel below the dairy, Homily, Pod and Peagreen were crammed behind

Arrietty in the Spiller Express. 'Hang on!' she yelled, and let the brake go.

They whizzed down the pipe and hurtled round a bend.

Meanwhile, Mr Potter's limo had stopped.

He sat in the back, fuming. A moment later Officer Steady walked slowly round the car, writing out a ticket. He was cheerful, smiling and in no hurry.

When he'd finished writing, he came to Mr Potter's window. 'Well, well, well,' he said genially. 'As those in the law enforcement line of business are inclined to say, we meet again, Mr Potter.' He blinked, looking at the cheese-glopped, foam-crusted, burned and torn-up lawyer. 'I'm sorry the face cream didn't work for you,' he added with sincere sympathy.

'What do you want?' Mr Potter growled.

'If I may offer a smattering of advice, sir? Try to be a little more cautious. Remember! Safety knows no season.'

'Just. Give. Me. The. Ticket,' Mr Potter said, teeth clenched.

'If you'd like to bear with me a moment, sir.

I'm afraid that the perforations on my ticket pad do not lend themselves to a speedy tear-away.'

Potter leaned forward and tapped Wrigley on the shoulder.

Wrigley put the car into reverse.

The limo knocked over the constable's bicycle and crushed it even flatter than Pete's. Then Wrigley put the car in first gear and ran over Officer Steady's bike again before roaring off.

Officer Steady watched, shaking his head. 'I'm beginning to dislike that gentleman,' he said.

The limo raced up the street, screeched around corners and ran through red lights. Wrigley didn't stop until they reached the Town Hall. He pulled up in front, and passers-by stared as the burned, tattered, cheese-encrusted lawyer climbed out. He dashed up the steps without looking right or left and hustled straight up the information desk.

'Quick,' he snapped. 'Where's Demolition? I need to register a house destruction.'

'What's the magic word?' the clerk asked.

Mr Potter glared. 'I'm in a hurry! I've got a house to demolish!'

'I'm waiting,' the clerk said politely.

'So am I,' Mr Potter snarled. 'Now, WHERE IS IT?'

The clerk shrugged. 'Go up the stairs. Take a right at the top. Straight on through the door. Climb four flights. I imagine you'll have to catch your breath at that point. Having done that, scuttle up four more flights, bear left and turn right at Sewage . . .'

Calmly the clerk went on to issue further instructions. Potter listened, his face getting more purple and his eyes bulging.

'. . . instead of the door to the right. Go eight steps, maybe four if you step big, and you'll see a fire escape on your left. There's a staircase next to it. Go up three more flights, down the hall, turn right at Construction and look for Demolition.' The clerk smiled. 'You can't miss it.'

'Isn't there a faster way?' Mr Potter demanded.

'Walk quickly,' the clerk suggested.

Mr Potter took off, muttering to himself.

Right then, Exterminator Jeff's van screeched to a halt outside the Town Hall. He and Pete raced inside the building and ran, panting, up to the clerk.

'Excuse me, ma'am,' Pete said politely. 'Could you please direct me to Demolition?'

The clerk gave him a polite smile back. 'Certainly, young man,' she said. 'Take the lift to the top and go straight ahead. You can't miss it.'

'Thank you,' Pete said.

'You're very welcome,' the clerk responded, and as Pete and Jeff hurried to the lift she nodded approval. 'Such a nice boy.'

When Mr Potter staggered at last on to the top floor, he rounded a corner and smashed into Jeff and Pete, who were standing outside a door.

'Aha!' the lawyer snarled. 'Gotcha, you midget-loving brat!' He grabbed hold of Pete, then turned to Jeff. 'What are you doing here?'

'Trying to stop you from doing a very bad thing,' Jeff said.

Mr Potter laughed as he shoved them backwards down the hall. 'You're going to stop me, are you?'

Pete nodded and Exterminator Jeff said, 'Enough is enough.'

'How, exactly?' Mr Potter asked, smiling smugly.

Pete and Jeff looked at each other as they backed up.

Jeff said, 'Uh, we didn't really think about that, did we?'

'I was kind of hoping it would just come to us,' Pete admitted.

Mr Potter shoved them into the lift and pressed DOWN.

Inside, Pete held up a screwdriver and said to Jeff, 'Keep your fingers crossed.'

SEVENTEEN

Mr Potter watched the lift door close and the light go on, indicating that the two inside were being taken back down. Then he stalked away.

'Left . . . right . . .' he muttered, looking at all the doors. 'When I take over this town, that clerk is going to be the first one to go.'

Then he saw a door marked DEMOLITION. 'Finally!' he exclaimed.

He rushed to the door and flung it open without bothering to knock. The door smashed into the wall and the sign swung down, revealing another sign beneath it that said SUPPLY ROOM.

Mr Potter was all ready to start making his demands, when he realized there wasn't a desk or a clerk. Instead, the room was filled with cleaning supplies. On the ceiling a fan twirled lazily.

'Nice try, kid,' he growled, and whirled around to leave – but just then the door clicked.

He was locked in.

'All right, who's in here?' he demanded.

No one answered.

Taking a step backwards, he realized too late that somehow his shoelaces had become tied together and he fell down with a thud.

Angrily he got up, then bent down to untie the knots.

High on a shelf behind him, a hatpin tied to a can of shoe polish was suspended from a string. Next to it was Pod, who gave a war cry and let the shoe-polish can go.

The hatpin sailed right down and jabbed Mr Potter a bull's-eye right on his bottom.

'YYYOOOOWWWWW!' Mr Potter jumped up.

On another shelf two bars of soap dangled in the air as counterweights. Peagreen and Homily were holding the other end of the line. When Homily gave Peagreen the signal, they both let go.

The bars of soap fell on to the nozzles of two cans of stinky insecticide. Both cans started spraying – right into Mr Potter's face.

'*Yaaaagh!*' he bellowed.

He grabbed his face, so he didn't see Arrietty and Pod launch themselves from a high shelf with rolls of tape worn round their waists. The tape unwound as Pod and Arrietty zoomed round and round the lawyer's head and upraised arms, taping him as they swung.

Then Pod landed on one of Mr Potter's shoulders and Arrietty on the other. Mr Potter blinked, making terrible faces, but his arms were taped and he couldn't do anything to get them.

'I hate you little people,' he snapped as Pod climbed down to Mr Potter's coat pocket.

'Got it,' Pod said, and held up the will.

Arrietty helped him back up on to the man's shoulder. Unseen by the Borrowers, Mr Potter was busy nudging his mobile phone out from a pocket.

'That will teach you to mess with Pod Clock,' Pod said.

Mr Potter sneered and with his elbow

squeezed a button on his cell phone. The aerial sprung up and cut through the tape.

'You were saying, *Señor* Clock?' Mr Potter said nastily as he freed his arms. First he snatched the will back and then he swept up all four Clocks in his other hand and dumped them on to the floor. He flipped over a wire rubbish bin, imprisoning them.

'Now for a suitable weapon of destruction,' he said as he looked along the shelves. 'Hah!' he shouted as he saw a vacuum cleaner.

The Borrowers, looking helplessly through the wire of their prison, gasped. A vacuum cleaner – their worst nightmare!

Cackling madly, Mr Potter turned it on and the machine whined into life. He poked the nozzle towards them, making a sucking noise with his lips. He laughed, then said, 'Nothing wrong with a little sucking up!'

'Hold on to the bars, everybody,' Pod yelled desperately.

The family gripped the wire of the rubbish bin, but the suction was too strong. Their bodies began to rise towards the nozzle as the hurricane-strong winds sucked at them.

But just when it seemed too late, the *wheeeennn!* of the machine died and the wind softened to a breeze, then stopped.

Mr Potter looked up. The ceiling fan had stopped turning – and as he watched, eight Borrowers, masked and dressed like ninjas, swung down on lines. Mr Potter looked down at his feet as the ninja Borrowers swiftly secured their lines to the floor with nails and tacks. They formed a circle all the way round him.

'What the . . .' Mr Potter demanded.

The trooper Borrowers raised their hands in a signal.

Two more outies switched the ceiling fan to FULL SPEED and the blades started to turn. Too late, Mr Potter realized what all those strings were for. *Whirrrr!* The ceiling fan blades blurred and the strings instantly wound round and round the angry lawyer, tying him up from nose to toes.

'Get . . . these . . . lines . . . OFF ME!' he screeched.

The fan did not stop. Instead, the Borrower team on the floor worked together to lift the rubbish bin so that the Clocks could crawl out.

Then the leader came forward and pulled off his mask – and there was a familiar, wild face.

'Spiller!' Arrietty cried happily. 'You're alive!'

'Nothing wrong with your eyesight then,' he said – but he was grinning too.

Arrietty threw her arms round Spiller and gave him a fierce hug. Three other members of the team came forward and also removed their masks.

'Blimey,' Pod exclaimed. 'It's Minty, Swag – and Dustbunny Bin!'

Minty pointed to Spiller. 'He said you were in trouble.'

Swag asked, 'Where've you been, Pod?'

'Yeah,' Dustbunny Bin said. 'We lost touch.'

Pod was so surprised he was unable to say anything. Homily stepped forward – and the three outies stepped back, frightened.

'Uh, hello, Mrs Clock,' Minty said.

'Well, Minty Branch,' Homily said briskly. 'It's quite obvious that you haven't changed one bit.' She hugged Dustbunny Bin and gave him a big kiss. 'And I'm so glad!'

Grunting and struggling noises from behind

claimed their attention. Mr Potter had almost wriggled free of the strings tying him.

'I'd keep still if I were you,' Spiller said.

'You think I'm afraid of twenty little creeps?' Mr Potter snarled. 'Ha! I'll squish you all!'

Spiller grinned. 'Twenty?' And he gave a sharp whistle.

Small shadows appeared on the walls.

From every shelf, box and piece of equipment, Borrowers began to appear. Young, old, dressed in forgotten scraps from every old house in the town, Borrowers came. Innies, outies, poor and rich. As Mr Potter and the surprised Clocks watched in growing wonder, more and more of them came, swinging down from the ceiling and joining the growing crowd moving steadily forward to ring the immobilized lawyer.

Near Arrietty a card file opened and five Borrowers popped up. From the vents more came. All around Mr Potter were hundreds – no, thousands – of Borrowers.

He looked frightened – but Arrietty looked around in awe, her whole face radiating happiness. Near Peagreen several Borrower boys appeared, all his age. He smiled at them shyly.

A hand tapped Homily on the shoulder. 'Homily, darling!'

Homily whirled round and saw a group of well-dressed, distinguished-looking Borrowers.

Several more Borrowers lowered a little lift down from the fan, which had stopped. The lift came to rest near Mr Potter's feet.

Minty said, 'Go on, Pod. It's your show.'

The thousands of Borrowers fell silent as Pod stepped forward.

EIGHTEEN

POD CAREFULLY WALKED INTO the lift, which was raised until he was even with Mr Potter's face.

'Listen, bean,' he said, looking steadily into Mr Potter's eyes. 'We're not vermin. We're not freaks. We're not pests. We're Borrowers.'

Behind him came a low murmur of approval from the thousands of watching Borrowers.

'Now, you might have thought that we Borrowers were a dying race. You might have thought that you human beans, with your concrete floors and your Central Eating, had driven us out of your houses and scattered our families far and wide. But you'd have been wrong. Look around you.'

He waved his hand at the Borrowers all lined

up silently on every surface, some of them carrying handmade weapons that had once been fountain pens or forks. All waited together in silence.

Pod continued, 'We Borrowers have been around just as long as beans and we mean to keep it that way. For we may be small to you, but heaven help any bean who thinks he can squish us.'

From the floor Arrietty looked up at her father, grinning in pride.

Pod said, 'We're Borrowers and proud of it. After all, a Borrower is quiet. Inconspicuous. Cautious. Alert. Honest. Friendly, but not overbearing. Ingenious. Brave. Timid but not afraid. Polite. Prudent. Attractive. A Borrower is dependable in a crisis. Resourceful. Romantic, but not sentimental. Faithful. Tolerant. Loyal. And we're very good at climbing . . .'

The crowd sent up a big cheer.

Swag and Dustbunny Bin exchanged looks and Swag whispered, 'Pod hasn't changed, has he?'

Dustbunny Bin grinned ruefully. 'He does love a chance to make a speech.'

Pod waved his finger at Potter's bright red

nose. 'Consider yourself "seen",' he said sternly. Then he turned and pointed at all the Borrowers. 'Look around you. Any more funny business and we know where to find you. Got it?'

All the Borrowers cheered again.

When the cheers died down, footsteps sounded outside in the hall: *clonk, clonk, clonk.* Thousands of Borrower heads whipped to face the door, which rattled as it was unlocked.

Officer Steady walked into the room and looked around. Pete was right behind him, scanning anxiously. They saw the lawyer standing alone in the middle of the room.

The lines were gone, and the tacks from the floor, and no one else was in the room. Mr Potter seemed to be all alone with a vacuum cleaner and boxes and shelves of cleaning stuff.

He opened his mouth. 'I've been seen,' he said in a tiny voice.

Pete reached forward and took the will from Mr Potter's pocket. Mr Potter didn't move. 'Here it is. I told you he had it,' he said in excitement. 'This proves he was trying to cheat us out of our house.'

Officer Steady quickly scanned the document. Then he gave Mr Potter a stern look, his cheer all gone. 'Anything to say in your defence, sir?'

Mr Potter said in that same small voice, 'Borrowers. Thousands of tiny Borrowers . . . Alert . . . Cautious . . .'

Officer Steady turned to Pete.

'Very good at climbing,' Mr Potter muttered, still in that weird voice.

Pete grinned and shrugged his shoulders, as if to say, 'He's crazy.'

Shaking his head, the constable pulled out a pair of handcuffs.

NINETEEN

NOT TOO MUCH LATER Mr Potter sat at a desk in the middle of the police station. He was still in his cheesy, foam-flecked, burned and torn suit, his hair standing up, his face a mess. He looked completely limp with defeat.

Officer Steady sat nearby. Other constables had stopped their work and were gathered in the background to listen.

'So,' Officer Steady said, 'little people, were they?'

Mr Potter looked around fearfully. 'That's what I've been trying to tell you,' he said. 'Millions of them!' He lowered his voice to a whisper. 'They're everywhere!'

Officer Steady said with a smile, 'I suppose

they have little houses, with little tables and little chairs?' He winked at his colleagues.

'Yes,' Mr Potter said slowly. 'They do.'

Everyone laughed.

Later that night, Officer Steady was sitting in the dining room at the old house. The Lenders had spent the day moving back in and cleaning up the mess. Things were still in boxes, awaiting the fixing of walls and repainting, but the candlelit table was full of good food and the house seemed cosy and warm, as if welcoming them back.

With Joe, Victoria, Pete and Officer Steady were Jeff and Mr Smelly. The dog lay happily on the floor, gnawing at a bone.

At the end of the dinner, Joe got to his feet. 'I just want to say a big thanks to you all for helping us save our house. We were a bit worried there for a while, but thanks to Pete and our new friends here, everything's looking rosy.'

Joe blinked. He felt his nose, his pockets and then squinted down at the table. 'Well,' he said sheepishly, 'at least things would look rosy if I could find my glasses . . .'

Then he shrugged and lifted his wine goblet high. 'Thank you!' he said.

Everyone cheered. The adults drank their wine and Pete drank hot chocolate. Mr Smelly gave a bark, then went back to his scraps.

Officer Steady got up and bowed to everyone at the table. 'And thank you, Mrs Lender, for a delicious and nutritionally balanced meal.'

Victoria smiled at Pete, who helped himself to seconds. 'All this excitement's certainly given Pete an appetite,' she said. 'I don't know where he's putting it!'

The adults all laughed at the joke. That is, all the adults except Jeff, who winked at Pete, then went back to his dessert.

Pete quickly grabbed some peas off his plate, then he slid off his chair and went to the hallway. There, he knelt down and dropped the peas, one by one, through a hidden trapdoor in the newly repaired floor.

Below the floor Peagreen stood by the cooker, catching the peas in his hands as they fell from Pete's fingers. He arranged them neatly on a large coin.

Beyond him the Clocks and their friends were

gathering in a large circle. They too still had their things piled about them, but the table was cosy and full of good food – thanks to Pete.

Pod was busy carving a shrimp. At his right sat his three old outie friends, Minty, Swag and Dustbunny Bin. They raised thimbles full of drink and roared with laughter as each told stories about their shared past.

'Do you remember when we borrowed that briefcase?' Dustbunny Bin asked.

'No, no,' Swag insisted, 'it was a handbag.'

Dustbunny Bin smacked his head. 'Oh yeah, of course. I meant a handbag.'

Minty shook his head. 'Wasn't it a brief-case?'

Homily put some shrimp on to each plate. 'No,' she said briskly. 'It was a wallet. I remember as clear as yesterday.'

'A wallet!' Minty, Swag and Dustbunny Bin said together. 'That's right!'

They all laughed.

Peagreen brought the peas over and set them on the table. 'So, Dad,' he asked, 'why'd you give up being an outie?'

'I've always thought it was best to do exactly

what your mother told me to do.' He smiled at Homily.

Dustbunny Bin, Swag and Minty raised their thimbles again and cheered noisily. Homily smiled back, cutting her food into ladylike bits.

Arrietty and Spiller, at the other end of the table, exchanged a look. Then they put down their forks, got up and headed for the door.

Homily looked up. 'Where are you two off to?'

'Just going for a walk round the garden, Mum,' Arrietty said.

Pod nodded. 'All right, love, have a nice time.'

'We will,' Arrietty said. She turned away to hide a grin.

Once they were out of sight of the others, Spiller pulled out two hidden walnut-shell helmets and off they headed for the Spiller Express.